NERDING OUT ABOUT
JAPANESE POPULAR CULTURE

NERD CULTURE

VIRGINIA LOH-HAGAN

45TH PARALLEL PRESS

Published in the United States of America by Cherry Lake Publishing Group
Ann Arbor, Michigan
www.cherrylakepublishing.com

Reading Adviser: Beth Walker Gambro, MS, Ed., Reading Consultant, Yorkville, IL
Book Designer: Joseph Hatch

Photo Credits: © Lightfield Studios, Adobe Stock, cover, title page; © enchanted_fairy/Shutterstock, 4; Toho Company Ltd. (東宝株式会社, Tōhō Kabushiki-kaisha) © 1954, Public domain, via Wikimedia Commons, 7; © Puiipouiz/Shutterstock, 8; Laika ac from UK, CC BY-SA 2.0 via Wikimedia Commons, 10; National Archives and Records Administration, Public domain, via Wikimedia Commons, 12; Cloud atlas, CC BY-SA 4.0 via Wikimedia Commons, 15; 朝日新聞社, Public domain, via Wikimedia Commons, 16; © Polin J Polin J/Shutterstock, 19; © Thongden Studio/Shutterstock, 21; © BlurryMe/Shutterstock, 22; 李 承儒, AKB48-Taiwan Clubs (ATC) 社長 (李 承儒's facebook page, flickr account link screenshot taken from the facebook page), CC BY-SA 2.0 via Wikimedia Commons, 24; © Lina Lobanova/Shutterstock, 26; © cfg1978/Shutterstock, 28; Kanko* from Nagasaki, JAPAN, CC BY 2.0 via Wikimedia Commons, 29

45th Parallel Press is an imprint of Cherry Lake Publishing Group.

Library of Congress Cataloging-in-Publication Data

Names: Loh-Hagan, Virginia, author.
Title: Nerding out about Japanese popular culture / Written by: Virginia
    Loh-Hagan.
Description: Ann Arbor : 45th Parallel Press, [2024] | Series: Nerd culture
    | Audience: Grades 4-6 | Summary: "Nerding Out About Japanese Popular
    Culture covers the wonderfully nerdy world of Japanese popular culture:
    from anime to J-Pop. This 45th Parallel hi-lo series includes
    considerate vocabulary and high-interest content"-- Provided by
    publisher.
Identifiers: LCCN 2023035082 | ISBN 9781668939352 (paperback) | ISBN
    9781668938317 (hardcover) | ISBN 9781668940693 (ebook) | ISBN
    9781668942048 (pdf)
Subjects: LCSH: Japan--Social life and customs--Juvenile literature.
Classification: LCC DS821 .L593 2024 | DDC 952--dc23/eng/20230808
LC record available at https://lccn.loc.gov/2023035082

Cherry Lake Publishing Group would like to acknowledge the work of the Partnership for 21st Century Learning, a Network of Battelle for Kids. Please visit Battelle for Kids online for more information.

Note from publisher: Websites change regularly, and their future contents are outside of our control. Supervise children when conducting any recommended online searches for extended learning opportunities.

Printed in the United States of America

Dr. Virginia Loh-Hagan is an author and educator. She is currently the Director of the Asian Pacific Islander Desi American (APIDA) Center at San Diego State University and the Co-Executive Director of The Asian American Education Project. She lives in San Diego with her very tall husband and very naughty dogs.

TABLE OF CONTENTS

Many Japanese popular culture nerds love anime shows like *Dragon Ball Z.*

LIVING THE NERDY LIFE

It's finally cool to be a nerd. Nerd culture is everywhere. It's in movies. It's on TV. It's in video games. It's in books. Everyone is talking about it. Everyone is watching it. Everyone is doing it. There's no escaping nerd culture.

Nerds and sports fans are alike. They have a lot in common. Instead of sports, nerds like nerdy things. Magic is nerdy. Science fiction is nerdy. Superheroes are nerdy. Nerds obsess over these interests. They're huge fans. They have a great love for a topic. They learn all they can. They spend hours on their hobbies. Hobbies are activities. Nerds hang with others who feel the same.

Nerds form **fandoms**. Fandoms are nerd networks. They're communities of fans. Nerds host online group chats. They host meetings. They host **conventions**. Conventions are large gatherings. They have speakers. They have workshops. They're also called **expos**. Tickets sell fast. Everyone wants to go. Nerd conventions are the place to be.

Nerd culture is on the rise. It's very popular. But it didn't used to be. Nerds used to be bullied. They were made fun of. They weren't seen as cool. They'd rather study than party. This made them seem odd. They were seen as different. Not anymore! Today, nerds rule!

Fascination with Japanese culture is nothing new. The movie *Godzilla* was popular around the world when it came out.

Japan's capital is Tokyo. Tokyo is modern and traditional.

CHAPTER 1

A CULTURE OF CUTENESS

Pop culture stands for popular culture. It's the culture of a community. It consists of cultural products. Examples are music, art, movies, books, and food. Pop culture reflects what's trendy. What's trendy changes. People's tastes change. Their interests change. This causes pop culture to change.

Different generations have their own pop culture. Different countries have their own pop culture. Japan is a country. It's in Asia. Japanese pop culture is hot. It has millions of fans. Its fans are all over the world. Fans love Japanese characters. They love Japanese products. They collect things. They spend a lot of money.

Hello Kitty cafes are all over the world.

Japanese pop culture is based on cuteness. Everything has to be cute. *Kawaii* means cute. It refers to a type of look. It's a culture of cuteness. It includes cute fashion. It includes cute cartoons. Pikachu is an example. Hello Kitty is an example. Hello Kitty is a **pop icon**. Pop icons are stars. They represent a culture. Hello Kitty represents Japanese pop culture.

Teens made *kawaii* culture popular. They used cute handwriting styles. They wrote in round letters. They wrote like children. They added hearts and stars. This style took off. It showed up everywhere.

The Pearl Harbor attack was a surprise.

CHAPTER 2

FROM MILITARY TO MEDIA

Japan wanted to be powerful. For many years, it invaded other countries. It wanted military power. In 1941, Japan attacked Pearl Harbor. Pearl Harbor is a U.S. Navy base. It is in Hawaii. The attack angered the United States. The United States entered World War II. It fought against Japan.

World War II was from 1939 to 1945. The United States dropped bombs in Japan. Japan lost the war. This stopped Japan's invasions.

Japan struggled. The war destroyed Japan. Japan became poor. It wasn't allowed to have a military. It was seen as an enemy. It had to rebuild. It needed a new image.

NERD LINGO!

OBAKE
Obake and *bakemono* refer to ghosts and monsters. They mean things that change. They're featured in Japanese folklore. They may also appear in Japanese pop stories.

OTAKU
Otaku is a person obsessed with Japanese popular culture. *Otaku* especially love anime. In Japan, this is a bad word. Being *otaku* means being lazy. *Otaku* seem to lack social skills. In the United States, *otaku* describes hardcore anime fans. It's not a bad word.

PURIKURA
Purikura means print club. They're Japanese digital photo sticker booths. People sit in booths. They take pictures. They add cute features. They led to the trend of selfies.

WEEB
Weeb is short for weeaboo. It means wannabe Japanese. It refers to non-Japanese people who love Japanese things. It can be an insult.

YURU CHARA
Yuru Chara are mascot characters. They're created to promote something. They promote businesses. They promote cities. They promote events. They're symbols. They're cute.

Postwar youth wanted something new. They wanted to be happy. They wanted to be seen. They embraced *kawaii* culture. They sold cuteness to all.

TV became popular. Everyone had a TV. Japan used TV to change its image. The Japanese created shows. They made movies. They made music. They also made toys. Toys were a big part of pop culture. Japan made many products.

Japan moved away from military power. It focused on media power. It created new idols. It created new icons. This let Japanese people see themselves. It let them see themselves differently. Pop culture focused more on youth. This ensured a strong future.

Popular postwar toys were toy cars. These cars were made from used cans.

Osamu Tezuka (1928–1989) created *Astro Boy*. He's the father of manga. He's like the Japanese Walt Disney.

CHAPTER 3

POPPIN' EXAMPLES

There are different examples of Japanese pop culture. Manga is one. It's one of the most popular.

Manga means whimsical drawings. Manga are Japanese comic books. They're graphic novels. Early versions of manga started in the 8th century. They showed animals acting like humans. They were printed on **scrolls**. Scrolls are rolls of paper.

Manga was printed in newspapers. Then they became books. Manga are read right to left. Many manga are series. They have many volumes.

Doujinshi is manga **fan fiction**. Fan fiction is written by fans. Fans write stories. They are based on existing manga characters.

NERD TO KNOW!

Yoko Kamio was born in 1966. She is Japanese. She creates manga. She draws. She writes. She created *Hana Yori Dango*. This translates to "Boys Over Flowers." It is the best-selling girls manga series of all time. It set world records. It has the most published copies of a single author. More than 61 million copies have been sold. It has been translated into different languages. It's been published in Asia, Europe, and North America. It's been turned into an anime series. It's been turned into movies. It's been turned into TV shows. Kamio has earned many awards. But she didn't mean to be a manga star. She started as a waitress. She went to school to be a secretary. She started drawing. She loved it. She started making manga. She created *Hana Yori Dango* in 1992. The story is about high school life. It's set in an elite school for rich people. It's about bullying. It's been described as *Gossip Girl* meets *Survivor*.

Manga is print. Many manga stories became popular **anime** shows. *Anime* is animation from Japan. It includes TV shows and movies.

Anime is a special art style. Characters have large eyes. They have facial expressions. Their hair is bright. Bold colors are used.

Anime shows started to release in the United States. This was in the 1960s. One show was *Astro Boy*. Another was *Speed Racer*. Japanese pop culture gained popularity. Anime fan clubs formed. Anime conventions took place. Many fans dressed up. They went as their favorite characters. This is called **cosplay**. Cosplay means costume play. It's a performance art.

Studio Ghibli is a Japanese animation studio. Its mascot is Totoro. Totoro is very famous.

Kaiju refers to Japanese monster movies. These monsters are big. They attack cities. They fight the military. They fight other monsters. *Kaiju* movies use special effects. The first *kaiju* movie was *Godzilla*. It was made in 1954. Godzilla represented **nuclear weapons**. Nuclear weapons use energy to explode. They're dangerous. Godzilla represented the bombing of Japan. It reflected postwar Japan. Many movies were made about Godzilla. Many movies were made about other giant monsters.

Japanese horror movies are also popular. American horror often focuses on violence. They focus on gore. But Japanese horror focuses on thrillers. Japanese movies focus on mind games. They're unsettling. They feature ghosts and spirits.

American filmmakers like Japanese film. Some have remade Japanese horror films.

Japanese video games are a big hit. Nintendo is the top Japanese video game company.

Arcades are indoor game centers. They have game machines. People pay money to play games. They win prizes. They win points. Japanese arcade culture is popular. It started in the 1980s. Arcades are in malls. They're in restaurants. Arcade culture spread around the world.

Game **consoles** were invented. Consoles are devices. They let people play games at home. Arcade culture declined. But not in Japan. Japanese gamers still play at arcades.

There are many types of games. There are video games. There are racing games. There are fighting games. There are crane games. The most popular are rhythm games. Rhythm games have players move. They move to a beat. They combine music with gameplay. *Dance Dance Revolution* is an example.

J-pop is Japanese pop music. Modern J-pop boomed in the 1990s. It has traditional Japanese music roots. It has Western influences. It combines pop and rock music. It mixes in electronic music. It also includes hip-hop. J-pop is in anime. It's in video games. This helped make it trendy.

There are J-pop singers. There are J-pop bands. J-pop artists are famous. They dance. They sing. They look cute. Fans love them. They created an **idol** culture. Idols are greatly admired. They're stars. Fans worship J-pop singers. They dress like them. They buy their music. They go to their concerts.

J-pop emerged in the 1960s. The girl group AKB48 is very popular.

TOO NERDY!

Maid cafés are cosplay restaurants. They're special coffee shops. They have anime and manga themes. They look like dollhouses. They're popular in Japan. Waitresses dress in maid outfits. They look cute. They act as servants. Fans of Japanese pop culture go there. They like being served by their favorite characters. The waitresses play games. They do arts and crafts. They sing. They dance. They serve food. They decorate food with cute designs. They shape rice into cute shapes. Maid cafés have rules. Customers can't touch the waitresses. They can't take pictures without asking. Waitresses can't share their names. They act their parts. A waitress said, "In the space of the café, we can be cute or whatever. But outside, we can be who we are in real life." The first permanent maid café opened in 2001. It's called Cure Maid Café. It's in Tokyo. Today, there are maid cafés all over the world.

Some people think cosplay is fan art. Fans who cosplay create their costumes based off of their favorite characters.

CHAPTER 4

RELEASE YOUR INNER NERD

You, too, can be a nerd for Japanese pop culture! Try one of these activities!

MAKE FAN ART!

Many fans love anime. They love manga. They have favorite characters. They draw these characters. They make **fan art**. This makes them fan artists.

Fan artists make drawings. They make paintings. They make sculptures. They make videos. They make **digital** art. This is made using a computer.

Fan artists share their work. They share it with other fans. They make art for themselves. They make art for fun. They can't sell it. This is because they're copying art. They don't own the original art. Fan artists need to respect the creators.

START AN ANIME CLUB!

Gather anime fans. Host watch parties. Watch anime together. Talk about it. Discuss your favorite characters. Discuss the plot. Discuss the art.

Most anime is in Japanese. Characters will speak in Japanese. Decide to "sub versus dub." Sub means to watch with **subtitles**. Subtitles are captions. They're at the bottom of screens. They write out what characters are saying. The **audio** will be in Japanese. Audio is sound. Fans read the subtitles.

Dubbed refers to voice-overs. English is dubbed over the Japanese. Fans can listen to anime in English. The lip movements might not match.

Some fans form manga book clubs. They read the same manga. Then they talk about it.

Japanese is written vertically, from top to bottom.

LEARN JAPANESE!

Loving Japanese pop culture includes loving Japan. Fans should not **appropriate**. This means taking another's culture for your own. Fans should **appreciate** Japanese culture. Appreciate means seeking to learn. It means seeking to understand. Fans should study Japanese history. They should study Japanese customs.

Superfans learn to speak the Japanese language. They experience Japanese pop culture differently. They experience it in its original language. Anime and manga are in Japanese. J-pop songs are in Japanese. Products have Japanese writing. Think about taking classes. Watch videos. Listen to J-pop. Practice making Japanese sounds. Practice with other Japanese speakers.

NERDY TIPS!

TIP #1

PRACTICE DRAWING BODIES.
MANGA AND ANIME ARTISTS
STUDY FIGURE DRAWING.
THEY KNOW HOW BODIES
ARE SHAPED. THEY KNOW
HOW BODIES WORK. THEN,
THEY EXAGGERATE SHAPES.

TIP #2

STUDY IMAGES.
USE IMAGES AS REFERENCE. DON'T
DRAW FROM MEMORY. BE CAREFUL
NOT TO COPY. DON'T STEAL THE
WORK OF OTHER ARTISTS.

TIP #3

LEARN WAYS TO DRAW SOUNDS. MANGA HAS SOUND EFFECTS. JAPANESE HAS MORE SOUND WORDS THAN ENGLISH DOES. SOUNDS ARE USED TO SHOW FEELINGS.

TIP #4

TAKE YOUR TIME READING MANGA. THERE'S A LOT GOING ON. READERS MUST INTERPRET SYMBOLS. THEY MUST LEARN CULTURAL REFERENCES. THEY MUST APPRECIATE CULTURAL DIFFERENCES.

TIP #5

VISIT JAPANESE AMERICAN COMMUNITIES. THEY'RE OFTEN CALLED LITTLE TOKYO OR JAPANTOWN. MANY HAVE SHOPS. IF YOU CAN, GO TO JAPAN. AKIHABARA IS IN TOKYO, JAPAN. IT HAS A LOT OF ANIME AND MANGA SHOPS.

GLOSSARY

anime (A-nuh-may) a style of Japanese film and television animation

appreciate (uh-PREE-shee-ayt) to seek to learn and understand another's culture

appropriate (uh-PROH-pree-ayt) to take another's culture or elements from that culture for personal interests

arcades (ar-KAYDZ) places to play games on money-operated machines

audio (AW-dee-oh) sound

consoles (KAHN-sohlz) electronic devices that output a video signal or image to display a video game that can be played with a game controller

conventions (kuhn-VEN-shuhnz) large meetings of fans who come together to talk about and to learn more about a shared interest

cosplay (KAHZ-play) the practice of dressing up as a character from a movie, book, or video game

digital (DI-juh-tuhl) created by using a computer

dubbed (DUHBD) added sound effects or new dialogue to movies or shows

expos (EK-spohz) large public exhibitions

fan art (FAN ART) art created by a fan and featuring characters from pop culture

fandoms (FAN-duhmz) communities of fans; combines "fanatic" and "kingdom"

fan fiction (FAN FIK-shuhn) stories written by fans based on characters, settings, and plots from other stories

idol (IYE-duhl) an object or person of extreme devotion

kawaii (kuh-WYE) the quality of being cute

nuclear weapons (NOO-klee-er WE-puhnz) bombs or missiles that use nuclear energy to cause an explosion

pop culture (PAHP KUHL-cher) short for popular culture, the cultural products of a society or generation that include music, art, movies, literature, and food

pop icon (PAHP IYE-kahn) a celebrity, character, or object regarded as a defining characteristic of a given society or era

scrolls (SKROHLZ) ancient books that were printed on rolls of paper

subtitles (SUHB-tie-tuhlz) captions at the bottom of a screen that translate what people are saying

LEARN MORE

Inzer, Christine Mari. *Diary of a Tokyo Teen: A Japanese-American Girl Travels to the Land of Trendy Fashion, High-Tech Toilets and Maid Cafes*. Tokyo: Tuttle Publishing, 2016.

Loh-Hagan, Virginia. *A is for Asian American: An Asian Pacific Islander Desi American Alphabet*. Ann Arbor, MI: Sleeping Bear Press, 2022.

Nakaya, Andrea C. *The History of Anime and Manga*. San Diego: ReferencePoint Press, 2022.

INDEX